The Usborne
Outdoor
Book

The
Usborne
Outdoor
Book

Written by Alice James and Emily Bone

Illustrated by Briony May Smith

Designed by Helen Edmonds and Anna Gould
Outdoor consultant: Laura McConnell

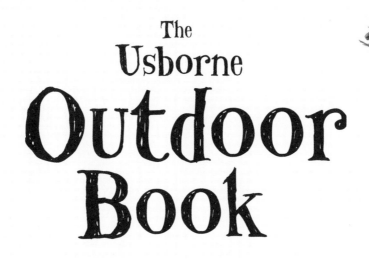

Contents

Usborne Quicklinks:

For links to websites where you can find out lots more about the outdoors, go to the Usborne Quicklinks website at www.usborne.com/quicklinks and enter the keywords 'outdoor book'.

Please follow the internet safety guidelines at the Usborne Quicklinks website. We recommend that children are supervised while using the internet.

The big outdoors

Wherever you are and whatever the weather, there are things to see, explore and do outdoors – whether that's just outside your house, in a park, by the sea or deep in the woods. No matter how far you're going, you should have an adult with you at all times.

How to use this book

This book is divided into sections, for different places and things to explore. These pages are from a section called 'Into the wild'.

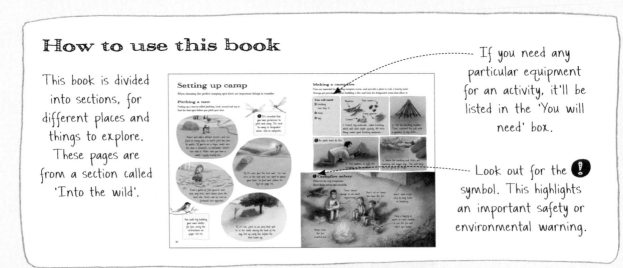

If you need any particular equipment for an activity, it'll be listed in the 'You will need' box.

Look out for the ❗ symbol. This highlights an important safety or environmental warning.

Getting outdoors is fun and easy – you don't need any specialized equipment.
But, if you're out all day or going far from your home, it's a good idea to be prepared.
Here are some useful things you might want to take with you.

A map

Tarpaulin to sit on, or for covering shelters

Something to eat

A sunhat if it's sunny

Water

❗ Staying safe

When you're outside, it's important to stay safe. Read the advice on pages 8-9 about protecting yourself – and the environment – while you're out and about.

Never go anywhere without a responsible adult.

Take a notebook and pencil with you to draw or make notes about plants and animals you see. To find out more about the things you spot, go to the Usborne Quicklinks website (see page 5).

❗ Someone in your group should carry a fully-charged phone at all times, in case of an emergency.

A waterproof coat if rain is on the way

A warm hat in case you get cold

Waterproof boots or shoes with lots of grip

One famous outdoor adventurer, Alfred Wainwright, said, "There is no such thing as bad weather, just bad clothing."

❗ Protecting nature

While you're outdoors, it's important to take care of the environment. Here are some tips:

Don't touch wild animals or their nests. You might damage them – or get stung or bitten.

If your path goes through farmland with animals, walk very quietly and calmly, so you don't scare them.

SHUT THE GATE

Don't pick any plants or flowers. You might kill the whole plant, and it's against the law in some places.

Follow local rules, such as shutting gates behind you, even if there is no sign. Always make sure you have permission to be outdoors. Remember, you're not allowed to go everywhere.

Put things back where you found them, take your litter away, and leave everything as you found it.

Some of the sections in this book show you how to catch small creatures for a closer look. Always put them back where you found them, carefully, in a sheltered spot.

⚠ Exploring safely

If you're out in the countryside, or by rivers or seas, you should follow this advice to stay safe.

Don't go near water in stormy weather, as waves can be very high and rivers can flood quickly. Tides can come in very quickly, too.

If you don't know how deep water is, don't step into it.

Rocky slopes and steep banks can be slippery and unstable, so avoid climbing on them.

Always have an adult with you.

Carry a bottle of water. Don't drink from streams or rivers – they might contain bacteria that could make you sick.

Stay on paths and tracks to keep to a safe route, and avoid harming plants or animals.

If it's going to be sunny, always wear sunscreen.

Over two-thirds of the world's surface
is covered in water, and all plants and
animals need water to survive.
This makes it one of the best places to
spot wildlife.

Exploring ponds, rivers and seas

Riverbanks and seashores are home to all kinds of creatures and plants. They're also great places to study how water moves and flows. The following pages are full of games and activities to try near water.

Seas

☆ Bounce a stone

☆ Track the tide

☆ Catch a crab

☆ Explore a rock pool

☆ Play seashore games

Ponds and rivers

☆ Dip for creatures

☆ Build a dam

☆ Race sticks under a bridge

☆ Build a mini raft

☆ Find out the depth of a river

On the seashore

Whether it's exploring a pool, catching a crab or hunting for things on the beach, there are lots of things to look for by the sea.

Rock pools

Rock pools or tide pools are small pools on the seashore. Here are some of the different creatures you might spot in them.

Try rock pool dipping, using the instructions for water dipping on page 18.

Mussels

Sea anemone

Edible crab

Shrimp

Crabbing

Use bait to catch a crab from a pool so you can take a closer look.

You will need:

☆ a piece of string at least as long as your arm

☆ a small stone or pebble

☆ crab bait – a small piece of bread, cheese, fish or bacon

☆ a bucket filled with sea water and placed in the shade

1. Tie some bait and the stone to one end of the string. Loop the other end over your finger.

2. Lower the bait into the water. You'll feel a tug when a crab is nibbling the bait. Slowly and gently start pulling up the line.

3. Place the crab in the bucket to look at it. Then, carefully pour the crab and water back into the pool.

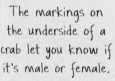

The markings on the underside of a crab let you know if it's male or female.

Male

Female

Seashore hunt

Wait until low tide and take a walk along the shore.
Look down to find out what the sea has washed up.

Write a list, take a
picture, or make a sketch
of what you've seen.

Don't take away things
you spot on a beach –
they might be home to a
sea creature.

Look for stones with
interesting shapes or markings.

See how many different
types of shells, driftwood
or seaweed you can find
on your hunt. If you can,
try to find out who lived
in the shells, too.

Seaweed

Shells of sea snails called
common periwinkles

Bone of a sea
creature called a
cuttlefish

Driftwood is wood
washed up by the sea.

An abalone is a large
sea snail with a
shiny shell.

On the sand

Marks on the sand might mean
that a creature has been there,
or there's one buried below.

Sand crab tracks

Lugworms are large worms that
live on the beach. They leave
these shapes as they burrow
under the sand.

These are burrows of sandhoppers
– creatures that live in the sand
during the day, then come out at
night to feed.

Footprint of
seashore bird

13

Seashore activities

When you're at the seashore, you can play games and learn about the tide, too.

Bouncing stones

Throw a stone across the sea and try to make it bounce off the surface as many times as possible before it sinks.

You will need:

☆ flat, round stones

☆ a calm sea without big waves

❗ Make sure there are no swimmers or animals in front of you before you bounce any stones.

Good bouncing stones are round, flat and smooth, like this.

1. Search the seashore for stones that will bounce well. Collect a few so you have a good supply.

2. Stand at the edge of the water. Hold a stone between your thumb and index finger, curling your finger around it.

3. Turn side-on to the sea and throw the stone, flicking your wrist to spin it at the same time.

Bouncing challenge

Challenge a friend to see who can get the most bounces after 10 throws. The world record for one throw is 88 bounces!

Sand darts

Using a stick or your finger, draw a big dot, the bull's-eye, in the sand. Then, draw five circles around it. Take a stone from the seashore. Walk five strides away from the outer circle. Try to throw the stone as close to the bull's-eye as possible.

Give each circle a score – 1 for the outer circle, then 2, 4, 6 and 10 for the bull's-eye. Each player has five throws, and the winner is the one with the highest score.

Fill a bucket

Divide into teams, with a bucket for each. Each team puts their bucket on the beach. Players take a beaker, then line up next to their bucket. One player shouts 'Go!' The first player in each team runs to the sea, fills their beaker, then races back to pour it into the bucket. The next person in the team goes, and so on. The first team to fill their bucket wins.

You will need:

☆ at least two teams of two or more people

☆ a bucket for each team

☆ a cup or beaker for each player

To make the game harder, you could use your hands instead of a cup or beaker.

Tracking the tide

If you spend a day at the beach, you'll notice that the sea is further from you, or closer to you, at different times. This is called a tide. The activity below shows you when the tide is going 'in' or 'out'.

1. When you get to the beach, put a marker, such as a stick, into the sand at the water's edge.

2. Check back 30 minutes later. If the stick is covered by water, the tide is going up the beach, or coming 'in'.

If it's dry and away from the water, the tide is going 'out'.

3. Put a marker at the water's edge every 30 minutes. If the sea starts to go in the opposite direction, you've reached 'low' or 'high' tide.

Low tide is the furthest the sea goes out. High tide is the furthest it goes in.

At the riverbank

Rivers flow all the way from mountains to the sea. If you spend time on a riverbank you can investigate the river and the variety of plants and animals that live there.

! Rivers can be dangerous. Always have an adult with you, and don't try to cross one. Stay away from steep banks, too (read the safety information on page 9).

Is the river straight and rocky with fast-flowing water, or winding, slow and deep? The slower and more winding a river is, the closer it is to the sea.

See if you can spot water birds and their nests.

Build a mini raft (find out how on the opposite page).

You can make a tool to test the depth of a river. Try it out at different places along the river, using the steps below.

Look for plants and animals in the water and on the bank.

How deep?

You will need:

☆ a stick

☆ a piece of string as long as your leg

☆ a small stone

1. Tie the string to the stick. Then, tie the small stone to the end of the string.

2. Lower the stone into the river until it touches the bottom. Lift it out again. If it doesn't reach the bottom then the river is very deep.

Wet to here

3. The wet part of the string shows the depth of the river.

Twig rafts

Build a mini raft from twigs and string, then float it on the water.
You could also add a deck and sail to turn it into a little boat.

You will need:

☆ four twigs

☆ four pieces of string

☆ scissors

☆ bark, moss and leaves

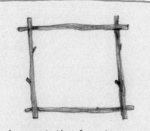

1. Lay out the four twigs in a square.

2. Tie the first piece of string around one twig, near one of the corners.

3. Wrap the string around the two twigs twice, like this.

4. Wrap the string twice the other way, too. Then, tie the two ends of string together to secure them. Trim off any excess string.

5. Do the same at each corner. Then, put your raft on the water. Which way is the river flowing?

Here are some ideas for turning rafts into boats:

Make a double leaf sail.

Tie more sticks onto the raft to fill the base.

Some leaves might make better sails than others. Experiment with big stiff leaves or several small leaves. Which makes the boat travel fastest?

Add a moss covering.

Find a piece of bark to make a deck.

Dipping and damming

If you're by a river or pond, you could try to find out what creatures live under the water. See what happens when you build a dam, too.

Water dipping

Dip a net into the water and move it in a small circle. Lift out the net and pour out anything you catch into a tub to have a closer look.

You will need:

☆ a net

☆ a tub, such as an old ice cream tub, filled with pond water

Water strider

Lots of plants grow with their roots in the water.

Frog's eggs are called frogspawn.

Water snail

Most creatures shelter around the edges of a pond or river, hiding in plants.

They grow into tadpoles...

...which grow into baby frogs.

Shrimp

Make notes about the creatures you've caught, so you can identify them later.

Any wings or fins?

Number of legs

Shape of body

Small fish

❗ Carefully pour everything back into the water when you've finished, at a sheltered edge.

Damming a stream

You could try building a barrier of rocks and sticks across a stream to stop it from flowing. Choose a shallow stream that's not very wide, so you can easily walk across it and the dam will work. Once you've made a dam, dip for creatures in the pool and examine what's left on the bed of the stream.

You will need:

☆ a small stream

☆ logs, stones and sticks

☆ mud and leaves

1. Place logs and large stones in a line from bank to bank across the stream.

2. Add smaller sticks and stones until your dam is taller than the water.

3. Plug any remaining holes with mud, leaves or twigs, to make it watertight.

Mud and leaves plugging the gaps

A strong foundation of logs and big stones

Smaller sticks and stones

! Always break up the dam before you leave.

Are there any creatures or plants left on the bed of the stream?

Beavers dam rivers with sticks and mud to create pools to live in. The deep water protects them from predators.

Stick racing

Face the side of the bridge with the water coming towards you. Drop your sticks together. Then run to the other side of the bridge to see which stick flows out first.

The best racing sticks are long and heavy.

19

The best time to spot animals and bugs is the morning or evening, when they're active. You'll see most during summer, as many hide away in the cold winter months.

Discovering wildlife

The pages in this section tell you how to explore the wildlife around you. You can find out which creatures live nearby, and create places for them to feed, nest and shelter.

☆ Capture footprints at night

☆ Make a trap to catch bugs

☆ Create a nest for bumblebees

☆ Sow wildflowers

☆ Learn to identify different birds

☆ Make your own bird feeder

☆ Build a bird bath

To watch animals, it helps to wear dark and loose clothing, so you blend in with your surroundings and keep your shape hidden.

Hunting creatures

You don't have to go far to discover the animals around you. Here are some activities you can do near your house, or in your local park.

Bird

Deer

Footprint trap

Put down this simple trap to capture the footprints of creatures moving around at night.

Squirrel

You will need:

☆ a big shallow tray

☆ some sand or soil

1. In the evening, take your tray to a spot where animals might walk, then fill it with sand. The best places are by holes in fences or gates.

2. Leave the trap overnight and in the morning, see which animals have walked through it. Compare with the prints here to identify the ones you've captured.

Fox

Water bird

Wildlife watching

You don't have to set traps to see wildlife. Keep quiet on a walk, or find a sheltered area to watch from. If you don't recognize a creature, make some notes and look it up later on a website about local wildlife.

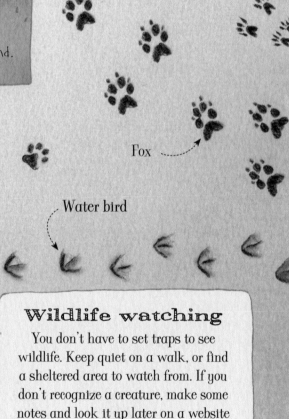

Cat

If you have a pond, put your tray near the water to pick up prints from water creatures, such as frogs or birds.

Bug traps

Set this trap to catch bugs, so you can get a closer look. Put anything you trap back where it came from carefully, by holding the cup next to the ground and waiting for the creature to crawl out.

You will need:

★ a trowel

★ a plastic cup

★ stones

★ a piece of wood or an old tile

1. Dig a small hole in soil and place the cup in it. Make sure the top of the cup is level with, or below the ground.

2. Put some stones either side of your hole and rest the wood or tile on top. Leave the trap alone for a few hours. Then have a look to see what you've caught.

Here are some tips to help you identify the types of bugs you have caught:

Beetle

A hard, shiny shell

Six legs

Millipede

A long body and lots of legs

Spider

Eight legs

Caterpillar

Long, hairy body. Some can be bright with striking patterns.

Slug or snail

Snails have a shell.

❗ Make sure you don't touch any animals you spot or catch, and never disturb a nest. Some will bite or sting if they feel threatened.

Ant

Small, dark body, and six legs

No legs, and a wet, slimy body

23

Encouraging bugs

You could create a bug-friendly area outside. Some bugs help plants to grow and others provide a tasty meal for birds and other animals.

Friendly flowers

Bees and butterflies feed on a sweet liquid inside flowers, called nectar. They visit flowers – including wildflowers and some herbs – with lots of nectar, or with nectar that's easy to reach. Try growing a container of bee- and butterfly-friendly plants. Look on these pages, research online, or ask your local garden store for ideas about which plants to grow.

Bees and butterflies spread a powder called pollen. This process is called pollination, and it makes flowers and seeds grow.

California poppy

Bee-friendly herbs include mint, marjoram or oregano, lavender and chives.

Lavender

Ox-eye daisy

Chives

A nest for bees

Use an upside-down flowerpot to make a nest for bees.

Fill a flowerpot with grass cuttings. Turn it upside down and half-bury it in soil or long grass.

You can grow many bee-friendly flowers from seed. Sprinkle a packet of your chosen seeds over compost. Then cover the seeds with another, thin, layer of compost. Water regularly.

Once you've set up the nest, don't touch it or look into it, as the bees might sting you.

Make a hole through a piece of orange using a pen or pencil. Push string through the hole and tie a knot.

Hang the string on a tree or bush. Butterflies will come and feed on the sweet juice.

Buddleia plants have lots of small flowers. Butterflies love to feed from purple buddleia, so it's known as the 'butterfly bush'.

Long grass

Letting grass and weeds grow creates feeding, nesting and hiding places for bugs and other creatures. Don't ever disturb overgrown areas.

Caterpillars feed on plants such as stinging nettles. Many birds eat caterpillars, too.

Dragonflies and damselflies rest on blades of grass.

Hiding holes

Give snails, frogs and other small creatures a damp hiding place.

Dig a small hole in the ground and half cover it with a small stone, brick or tile.

Old wood

Bark beetles and woodworms burrow into old, rotting wood.

Put old logs, stumps, or pieces of bark, in shady, damp corners.

Birdwatching

Wherever you are, there are different birds to watch, all year round. To identify a bird, look closely at its size, markings and other features. Make some notes or a sketch. You could find out more information online, including on the Usborne Quicklinks website (see page 5). Below are some things to look out for, to get you started.

A good starting point for identification is a bird's size. Does it look small and light, or big and powerful?

Beaks

Some water birds have long, curved beaks for hunting water creatures.

Birds of prey have hooked beaks for tearing meat.

Feathers

Are there any markings on the wings?

Does the bird have any bright or dark patches, or is it one shade all over?

Thick and pointed beaks are used by seed-eating birds.

Feet

Birds that eat seeds and insects only need small, thin feet.

Talons are strong, powerful feet with sharp claws for grabbing prey.

Some birds can be identified just by the way they fly. Look at the shape of their wings and watch to see whether they glide, flap or soar.

Water birds have webbed feet for swimming.

You can also encourage birds to visit using these ideas.

Make a feeder

Hungry birds will visit a bird feeder regularly, especially in winter and early spring. Here is an easy way to make one.

Cover a cardboard tube with peanut butter, then roll it in wild birdseed or sunflower seeds. Slot it over a branch...

...or tie string around it and hang it up.

Bird bath

Fill an old tray or plate with water and put it outside for birds to drink from and wash themselves in.

Add a twig or small branch for birds to stand on, so they can drink without getting wet and cold.

Put some gravel or sand in the bottom to make it look more natural.

Nesting material

In the spring, leave some of these materials in a sheltered spot for birds to build their nests with.

Small twigs

Moss

Fallen leaves

Grass cuttings

27

Trees grow layers on their trunks, which form in rings. One ring grows each year, so you can tell the age of a tree by counting its rings. Find a tree stump, and work out how old the tree was.

Tree rings

Investigating woods

Wherever trees grow – in woods or in cities – they are home to lots of living things, such as seeds, mushrooms, birds and insects. Discover how to identify different trees, fruits and seeds, as well as lots of other things to do in the woods.

☆ Identify trees

☆ Hunt for seeds, fruit and nuts

☆ Find creatures in and around trees

☆ Do a woodland obstacle course

☆ Make a trail for someone to follow

☆ Create a wild work of art

Tree detective

The easiest way to identify a tree is by examining its leaves. Find a leaf, look at its shape, edges and texture, then sketch it or make notes in your notebook. These examples give you ideas of what to look for.

Evergreen trees keep their leaves all year. They're normally thick and shiny, or shaped like needles.

Thick and shiny

Leaves with wavy edges, such as this oak, are known as lobed leaves.

Holly is an evergreen.

Some trees lose their leaves in winter. They're called deciduous trees.

Spiky edges with sharp points

Needle shape

Some leaves are spear-shaped with a ridged texture, such as beech.

Conifer trees have lots of tiny leaves clustered on a branch.

Some trees, such as ash, have small leaves spaced out along branches.

Some hand-shaped leaves have five 'fingers', like this maple, and some have three.

To find out more about which tree a leaf has come from, look online, or on the Usborne Quicklinks website (see page 5).

Hand shape

Seeds and fruit

From late summer, trees produce all kinds of seeds, nuts and fruit. These drop to the ground and eventually grow into more trees. Here are some different types you may find on the woodland floor.

Helicopters
Seeds from maples and some sycamores

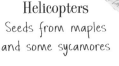

Helicopters spiral to the ground as they fall from trees.

Fruit
Soft, like plums and berries, or hard, like apples

Acorns
Nuts from oak trees

Pine cones
Large and spiky seed cases that grow on conifer trees

Conkers
Dark, shiny nuts covered in a prickly case, from horse-chestnut trees

Around the base

Lots of things live and grow on the damp base of trees or on fallen, dead ones, feeding on old bark and rotting leaves. How many different things can you spot around trees?

Woodworm holes

Lichen

A line of ants

Woodworms and beetles feed on the rotting wood.

Hole for a nesting owl

Trunk

Examine a tree trunk for signs of woodland creatures — nests, scratches in the bark or even the animals themselves.

Bark damaged by woodpeckers or squirrels looking for food or making a nest

Squirrel

Green moss

Mushrooms grow on moist bark at the base of the trunk.

Rabbits and other animals burrow between tree roots.

Obstacles and trails

Whether it's leaping over woodland obstacles or marking a trail, there are lots of different ways to explore the woods.

Woodland obstacle course

Obstacles such as fallen trees, stumps and puddles are everywhere in the woods. Here are some fun ideas for how to get over them. Keep to short, low or narrow obstacles, and look around you before you leap to make sure you don't get hurt.

Tree stump balance
Stand on a low stump on one leg, and try not to wobble.

Stump jump-up
Bend your knees with your arms straight behind you. Launch yourself up, swinging your arms forward, to land on top of the stump.

Fallen log vault
Run up to the log. Put both hands on it, then push yourself up and over.

Puddle leap
Take a run up and push off with one leg to leap over a big puddle. Land with the other leg.

Marking trails

If you're in a group in the woods, you could divide into two teams. One team marks a trail for the other team to follow, using signs. Here are some ideas for signs:

Turn left

Turn right

> Make your signs out of things you find in the woods, such as sticks or stones. Make sure each sign is big and clear, so that the other team won't miss it.

Over the fallen tree

Danger! Nettles or brambles

> Traditionally, these types of signs were used by trackers and explorers to tell each other where to go.

Not this way

> The best trails aren't too long or too complicated. Keep them simple and clear.

Natural signs

Another way to mark a trail is by using natural landmarks, such as fallen logs, patches of flowers, or distinctive trees. Go on a walk and make a list of landmarks you pass. Then see if the other team can use the list to navigate through the woods.

You could pile up stones to mark the finish.

Wild art

When you're in the woods, you could use the things around you to make wild works of art.

Wild piles

Sticks and stones can make interesting natural sculptures.

Collect together different stones, some large ones, some medium-sized and some small. Pile them up, with the largest on the bottom and the smallest on top.

You could place different stones in circles, like this.

Make a sculpture using sticks. Try to collect sticks that are the same size, then pile them up.

Walking art

Make patterns by using just your feet.

In mud or sand, make footprints, then go back and try to put your feet in exactly the same places to make the footprints deeper.

Make a pattern in long grass by walking the same path several times.

Try to come up with other ideas for wild art, that aren't on these pages.

Body shapes

If you're out with a friend, create art using sticks, stones, leaves and your bodies.

One person lies on dry ground with their arms and legs out. The other person places a line of sticks, stones and leaves around them, on the ground.

When they stand up, an outline of their body is left behind.

Leafy circles

Late in the year, collect together different kinds of leaves, then place them in circles to make patterns.

❗ Don't ever pick leaves while they're still on a tree.

This art is sometimes known as 'Land Art'. It's inspired by British artists Richard Long and Andy Goldsworthy, who make art from natural materials. To look at examples of their work, go to the Usborne Quicklinks website (see page 5).

Natural lines

You could create a striking line pattern by placing sticks onto the ground.

35

As part of their training, astronauts learn lots of the skills in this section — such as building shelters and fires — in case they crash-land in the wilderness.

Into the wild

Camping outdoors is a great adventure. Here you can find information about setting up a camp, from choosing the best position to pitch a tent, to building a campfire.

☆ Find the best camping spot   ☆ Navigate using the Sun

☆ Build a fire   ☆ Draw a map

☆ Cook a potato on the fire   ☆ Communicate using secret messages

☆ Construct a sturdy shelter

Knots are useful for all kinds of things when you're outdoors.
This knot is for tying a rope to a tree or post. Follow the steps
here and use it to build the shelters on page 41.

1.

2.

3.

Setting up camp

When choosing the perfect camping spot there are important things to consider.

Pitching a tent

Putting up a tent is called pitching. Look around and try to find the best spot before you pitch your tent.

Rivers and lakes attract insects and can flood in heavy rain, so don't pitch too close to water. If you're on a slope, make sure the door is downhill, so rainwater doesn't run into it. Make sure you have a water supply nearby too.

! It's essential that you have permission to pitch and camp. It's best to camp in designated areas, such as campsites.

If it's cool, face the tent east. The Sun rises in the east and can start to warm your tent. To find east, follow the tips on page 44.

Find a patch of flat ground and clear any sticks and stones from the tent site. Sticks can be used as firewood (see opposite).

You could try building your own shelter for fun, using the instructions on pages 40-41.

If it's hot, pitch in an area that will be in the shade during the heat of the day. Get up early too, before the tent heats up.

Making a campfire

Fires are essential for keeping campers warm and provide a place to cook a hearty meal. Always get permission before building a fire and look for designated areas that allow it.

You will need:
☆ kindling
(see step 1)
☆ sticks
☆ logs

Bracken

Pine cones

Long grasses

Leaves

1. Collect dry materials, called kindling, which will catch alight quickly. All these things make good kindling materials.

2. Pile the kindling together. Then, surround the pile with a pyramid of dry sticks.

An adult must do this:

3. Use matches to light the kindling in the middle.

4. When the kindling and sticks are burning, add bigger logs. This will keep the fire going for longer.

Campfire safety

Fires can be very dangerous. Read these safety tips carefully.

There should always be an adult supervising.

Don't sit or stand too near the fire.

Don't start a fire close to any tents or buildings.

Keep a supply of water or sand nearby to put the fire out when you leave.

Never leave the fire unattended.

Building a shelter

You can build your own shelter or den using sticks or just a rope and sheet.

Stick shelter

You can make a stick shelter using nothing but the logs and branches around you in the woods. It looks simple, but it's surprisingly stable and is used by wilderness explorers.

You will need:

☆ two forked branches

☆ one long branch

☆ lots of smaller sticks and branches

1. To make the entrance to your den, hold the two forked branches together in a wide triangle shape.

2. Carefully prop one end of the long branch onto the forked branches. Make sure the branches can stand up on their own.

3. Add lots of sticks to both sides, placing them one by one against the long branch, until the sides are covered. You'll need to hunt for sticks of different lengths.

If there are lots of extra twigs and leaves on the ground, you could use them to cover the sides of your shelter. Weave thin twigs between the sticks and put leaves on top.

See if you can crawl inside.

A-frame shelter

Tie a long piece of rope or heavy-duty string between two trees. Then, drape a tarpaulin or sheet over the top.

!Always take apart your shelter and clean up your camp before going home.

Use dry leaves to make a floor.

Stones are useful to weigh down the sides.

Arrowhead shelter

Tie one corner of a tarpaulin or a sheet to a tree trunk. Then, secure the opposite corner to the ground. Tuck in the sides to make a floor.

If the tarpaulin doesn't have any holes, wrap a small stone in the corner. Then tie the rope around the stone.

Tie the back corner to a tent peg or a pointed stick pushed into the ground.

Place stones on the inside to weigh down the tarpaulin.

Campfire cooking

When the flames of a campfire have died down and the logs are glowing with heat, that's the best time to cook some campfire food.

You will need:

☆ heavy-duty cooking foil
☆ a knife and spoon
☆ metal tongs
☆ oven gloves or mitts

❗ Even small fires can be extremely dangerous. Make sure you read the safety information on page 39 before making one.

All the flames should have died down.

The red part of the fire is called the embers.

The logs should be covered in white ash, and glowing red.

❗ Always wear an oven glove or mitt when handling hot food and only ever take things in and out of the fire using tongs.

Marshmallow cookie sandwich

Ingredients:

☆ marshmallows
☆ cookies
☆ skewers

1. Push a marshmallow onto the end of a skewer. Hold it above the fire for around 15 seconds, slowly turning it around.

2. Place the hot marshmallow, still on its skewer, on a cookie. Put another cookie on top and press them together. Then, pull out the skewer.

Fire-baked potato

Ingredients:

☆ a large potato

☆ butter or spread

1. Use a knife to slice the potato in half. Put a spoonful of butter or spread between the two halves and press them back together.

2. Wrap the potato halves tightly in foil. Using gloves and tongs, gently push the potato into the embers.

3. Leave it to cook for 20 minutes. Then, use tongs to turn it over. After another 20 minutes, take it out.

4. Wearing an oven glove or mitt, squeeze the potato. If it feels soft it's ready to eat. If not, put it back in until it's done.

5. Leave the potato to cool for 10 minutes. Unwrap it and eat straight from the foil. You could add some grated cheese too.

Corn on the cob

Ingredients:

☆ corn on the cob still in its husk (with its leaves on)

☆ butter or spread

1. Soak the corn in water for an hour.

2. Wrap the corn and its husk tightly in foil. Wearing gloves and using tongs, push it into the embers.

3. After 20–25 minutes, use tongs to take the corn out of the fire. Leave it to cool for ten minutes.

4. Carefully unwrap the foil and take off the leaves. Spread a teaspoon of butter or spread over the kernels and eat straight away.

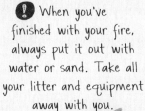

❗ When you've finished with your fire, always put it out with water or sand. Take all your litter and equipment away with you.

Finding your way

When you're out exploring, the Sun and landscape can help you find your way. But you should always carry a map, too.

Make note of landmarks that can be seen from a distance.

Setting Sun

The Sun and the Moon both rise in the east and set in the west.

Find north using the Sun

If it's a sunny day, you can use the movement of the Sun across the sky to find north.

You will need:

☆ a sunny, open space

☆ a straight stick or branch at least 1m (3ft) long

☆ two stones

1. Push your stick into the ground and place a stone at the very tip of its shadow.

First stone

2. Wait for 20 minutes. Use a second stone to mark the new position of the shadow on the ground.

3. Put your left foot against the first stone, and your right foot against the second. You are facing north.

4. Once you've found north, you can mark out other directions — south, east and west.

North

East

West

South

Make your own map

To map a place you've explored, all you need is paper, pens and pencils and your skills of observation.
A map can show a route for friends to follow, or reveal the locations of your campsites and hiding places.

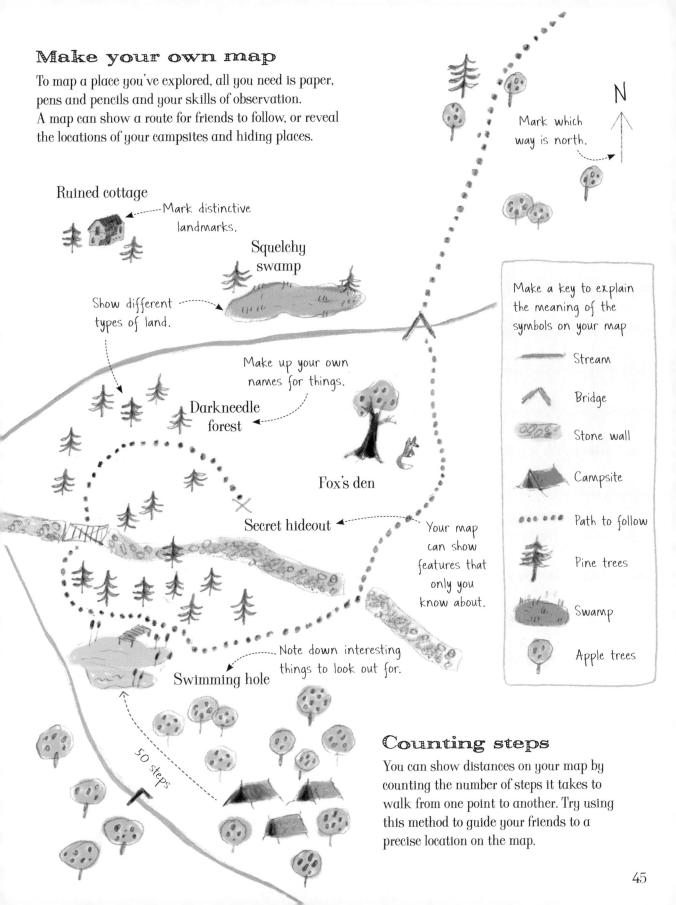

Mark which way is north.

N

Ruined cottage

Mark distinctive landmarks.

Squelchy swamp

Show different types of land.

Make up your own names for things.

Darkneedle forest

Fox's den

Secret hideout

Your map can show features that only you know about.

Note down interesting things to look out for.

Swimming hole

50 steps

Make a key to explain the meaning of the symbols on your map

— Stream

∧ Bridge

Stone wall

Campsite

• • • Path to follow

Pine trees

Swamp

Apple trees

Counting steps

You can show distances on your map by counting the number of steps it takes to walk from one point to another. Try using this method to guide your friends to a precise location on the map.

Sending messages

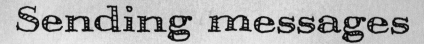

Learning how to send messages without words is a useful skill for outdoor adventurers, as it allows them to communicate over long distances. It's a fun way to send secret messages to your friends, too.

Morse code

In Morse code, each letter of the alphabet is turned into a series of dots and dashes. You can send a Morse message to someone else in the dark by turning a light on and off.

Position yourselves so you can see each other's flashes of light clearly.

⚠ Never shine your light directly into anyone's eyes.

You'll need a copy of the code and a notebook and pencil to decode the message.

- • A dot is a flash of light lasting one second.
- — A dash is a beam of light lasting three seconds.

Leave two seconds between letters, and five seconds between words.

The Morse alphabet

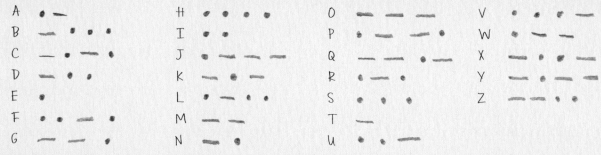

A • —	H • • • •	O — — —	V • • • —
B — • • •	I • •	P • — — •	W • — —
C — • — •	J • — — —	Q — — • —	X — • • —
D — • •	K — • —	R • — •	Y — • — —
E •	L • — • •	S • • •	Z — — • •
F • • — •	M — —	T —	
G — — •	N — •	U • • —	

Semaphore

Semaphore was traditionally used at sea to send messages between boats within sight of each other. The sender holds their arms in specific positions, which stand for different letters. It's usually done with flags, but you could wear gloves, or make 'flags' out of card.

Try spelling words, and then simple messages. Do you think it is easier or more difficult to understand than Morse?

A B C D E F G H I

J K L M N O P Q R

S T U V W X Y Z End of word

Your own wilderness language

Once you've mastered Morse and semaphore, use sounds or different body positions to make up your own secret codes. Here are some ideas to get you started:

Keep low

Animal ahead

"Hoot hoot!"

Pretend to stamp feet

Look out

Make sure each signal of your code is clear and different from the others so you can't get them mixed up.

47

Some people think that you can predict the weather by looking at the leaves on trees. If the leaves of deciduous trees such as maple and beech are curling up, it could mean rain is on the way.

Out in all weathers

Come rain or snow, there are still lots of things to do outdoors.

☆ Learn cloud names

☆ Predict the weather

☆ Measure rainfall

☆ Go on a soggy nature hunt

☆ Explore a snowy landscape

☆ Build an igloo

Rainbows appear when the Sun shines on water droplets in the air. You're likely to spot a rainbow when there is a heavy rain shower and the Sun is shining at the same time.

Cloud spotting

Stand outside, find a space where you can see the sky clearly and look up – whatever the weather, you're likely to see clouds. But there are actually lots of different types. Using the guide on these pages, start cloud spotting.

Cirrus
Wispy, white clouds, like strands of hair

Cirrostratus
A thin, white blanket across the sky, making the Sun look hazy

Nimbostratus
A thick, dark blanket of cloud

Thin lines like these are contrails. They're made by planes.

Stratus
A featureless, dull blanket of pale cloud low in the sky

Cumulus
Big, fluffy white clouds, with flat bottoms

Cumulonimbus
Tall, dark storm clouds
that stretch up into the sky

Cirrocumulus
Tiny, fluffy
white clouds

Altocumulus
Small, fluffy
white clouds

Cloud forecasting

Before the introduction of weather forecasts, people studied the clouds in the morning to predict what the weather would be like for the rest of the day. You could try this too. See how often your predictions are correct.

Stratus and nimbostratus

might mean drizzling rain or snow.

Cirrostratus

might mean drizzle, mist or fog.

Cirrus and altocumulus

might mean changeable weather.

Cumulus

might mean rain, if the clouds get bigger, or fair weather if they stay the same size throughout the day.

Cumulonimbus

might mean heavy rain, hail or even thunder and lightning are on their way.

! You should never look directly at the Sun, as it could damage your eyes.

51

Rain and snow

If it's raining or snowing, why not put on waterproof clothes and get outside? Here are some activities for a damp day.

Use the rainwater you collect in your gauge to water plants when it's dry.

Rain gauge

A rain gauge is a simple tool to measure rainfall. Leave it outside for a few days or a week to see how much rain has fallen where you live.

You will need:

☆ a tall plastic cup (use one with a domed lid with a hole in it if possible)

☆ small stones

☆ a marker pen

☆ a ruler

These will stop the cup blowing over.

1. Put stones in the cup, then pour in water to cover them. Place the lid on, upside down.

2. Starting at the water level, mark a scale up the cup, every cm or inch.

3. Put the gauge outside. After it rains, check the level of water.

Soggy creature hunt

Some animals love wet weather, so go hunting for bugs and beasts in the rain.

Birds hunt for worms and insects that come out when it rains.

Frogs breathe through their skin when it's wet, so they come out most on rainy days.

Worms go above ground when it's wet to crawl from place to place.

Snail.

Slug.

Snowy days

When the air gets very cold, the water in clouds freezes, then falls as snow. Snow can make familiar places look very different.

Snowflakes can be amazing shapes – no two are ever the same. Try looking through a magnifying glass to see them.

Icicles form when snow melts into drips of water, then freezes again.

When it's snowing heavily and very windy, snow can pile up against things in drifts.

If you see animal tracks in the snow, try to identify them using the prints on page 22.

Frost is made up of tiny frozen drops of water. It can make interesting patterns on plants and windows.

Mini igloo

If there is *a lot of* snow, you could build a mini snow house, known as an igloo.

You will need:

☆ plastic tubs, such as small ice cream tubs

☆ warm clothing, including gloves

1. Make snow bricks by scooping snow into the tubs, then pressing down, hard.

2. Build the base by placing the bricks in a circle.

3. Build more circles of bricks on top of the base, leaning each layer slightly towards the middle.

4. Use extra snow to close up the gaps.

5. Wedge in bricks to seal the top.

Sunny day games

Here are some outdoor games to play when you're in a group. They're most fun on a warm summer's day, but you can play them any time of year.

Hide together

One person is given 30 seconds to hide. Everyone else starts looking for them. Anyone who finds them hides in the same place. The last one still searching loses the game and hides next time.

Set a boundary, such as a small area in a park, or this hiding game becomes too difficult.

Limbo under a rope.

Obstacle course

Create an obstacle course from objects you have at home. Complete the course, then time other people in your group to see who can finish it the fastest.

Hop to the finish line.

You could use:

☆ rope or string
☆ buckets
☆ balls
☆ sacks or sheets
☆ hoops
☆ anything else you can find!

Climb through hoops.

Jump onto a stump.

Throw a ball into a bucket before moving on.

Scavenger hunt

One person makes a list of things to spot. Everyone takes a copy of the list and tries to spot each item. The first person to find everything on the list is the winner.

Only spot things. Don't pick them up or take them away.

The list could include things such as:

A statue

A round leaf

A wild animal, such as a squirrel

A dog

A bird

A water plant

Scavenger hunts are a great activity all year round. The things you're searching for will change throughout the seasons.

GO!

Guard the castle

Decide on an area to be the 'castle'. One person is the guard and counts to 30 while everyone else goes to hide. The guard shouts 'Go'. The hiders have to try to sneak back to the castle without being caught by the guard.

The 'castle' could be a tree, fence, or anything you want it to be.

The game is over when everyone has made it back to the castle, or been caught. Then someone else becomes the guard.

Animals that are active at
night are called nocturnal
animals. They come out
to catch prey. For some
animals in hot places, it's
also a way to stay cool.

Night explorer

Look and listen for creatures at night,
or do some stargazing.

- ☆ Listen for owls and foxes
- ☆ Hunt for fireflies
- ☆ Attract moths using light
- ☆ Follow slug and snail trails
- ☆ Learn constellations

- ☆ Look for planets and shooting stars
- ☆ Investigate the Moon
- ☆ Find north using the stars

Nature hunt at night

When you're going to sleep, some animals are only just waking up. If you have an adult to go with you, you could go on a nature walk at night to spot nocturnal creatures.

Night walk

Set out at dusk with a light and warm clothes. Stop every so often, turn off your light and wait a few minutes. What can you see and hear?

"Twit-twoo!"

"Hoot!"

Bats
Bats fly near water and meadows catching insects. Look for their dark, swooping bodies.

Owls
Owls fly low over grass hunting for food. It's easier to hear than see them.

Insects
Lots of insects are attracted to light. Look underneath streetlights and listen for buzzing wings.

"Croak!"

Some animals create their own light. In some areas you might see the pinprick lights of fireflies in hedgerows and long grasses.

Frogs and toads
Look for frogs and toads near water, in wet grass. Listen for their croaks as well.

"Howl!"

"Bark!"

Crickets are very loud at night. They make a chirping sound by rubbing their wings together very quickly.

Foxes
Foxes can live almost anywhere, in cities and the countryside. Listen out for their high-pitched calls.

58

Night light detective

A bright light is an easy way to find creatures at night.

Trapping moths

Drape an old sheet over a washing line or fence. Shine your light onto it and wait. Moths are attracted to the bright light, and will land on the sheet.

Look at the variety of moths you've trapped. See if you can identify any of them.

Have any other insects landed on your sheet?

Frogs' eyes shine green.

Cats' eyes shine yellow.

Foxes' eyes shine red.

Bright eyes

Animals' eyes reflect light. Shine a light across grass and shrubs. Do any eyes shine back?

Trails of slime

Snails and slugs leave slimy trails that will glimmer in your beam of light. Follow a trail to find the creature that's left it.

Snail trails are dotted.

Slug trails are continuous.

Stargazing

On a clear, cloudless night, look for stars, the Moon and even planets and shooting stars. It's easiest to see stars away from the bright lights of cities and towns. If you go out at night, make sure an adult is with you.

What you can see will depend on where in the world you are, and what time of year it is. Look online to see what should be visible on the night you want to stargaze.

Constellations

Early astronomers imagined stars as pictures, called constellations. Here are some well known ones from around the world.

This is a massive star called Betelgeuse.

Orion is shaped like a man with a shield and sword. He's named after a hunter in Greek mythology.

Bright stars

The brightest star in the sky is called Sirius, which means 'glowing' in Ancient Greek.

The bright North Star shines above the North Pole, so it always points north.

You'll find the North star just above the tip of the Plough, or Big Dipper.

In the Southern Hemisphere, Crux, also known as the Southern Cross, is always pointing south.

The Plough, or Big Dipper

How to stargaze

Wrap up warm and take a blanket with you. Find an open spot. It's most comfortable to sit or lie down. Then, look up. You can see more stars if you turn off any lights around you.

The Moon

The Moon is a huge lump of rock that moves around the Earth. It looks as if it's shining, but in fact, it's being lit up by the Sun.

This is a Full Moon.

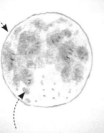

Dark patches are called *maria*. They were caused by lava from volcanic eruptions.

As the Moon travels round the Earth, the Sun lights up different parts of it. You can watch the Moon appear to change shape throughout the month.

Cresent Moon

Half Moon

Full Moon

Planets

You can tell planets apart from stars because stars twinkle and planets don't.

Mars has a reddish glow.

Jupiter looks like a big, bright star.

Venus is white. It often appears at dawn near the horizon, so it's known as the Morning Star.

Shooting stars

Shooting stars are actually space rocks, called meteorites, burning up in Earth's atmosphere. They look like long streaks of white in the sky.

Glossary

Here are some useful outdoor words used in the book that you might not know.

A-frame shelter - a shelter made with a sheet and rope, with sloping sides to keep off the rain.

altocumulus - small, fluffy white clouds.

Arrowhead shelter - a shelter made using a sheet and rope, that's open at just one end.

cirrocumulus - tiny, fluffy white clouds that form high in the sky.

cirrostratus - a white blanket of cloud across the sky. It makes the Sun look hazy.

cirrus - wispy, white clouds.

compass - a tool that uses a magnet and needle to find north.

constellation - a pattern of stars in the night sky.

contrails - white lines in the sky made by planes.

Crescent Moon - when only a small section of the Moon is lit up in the night sky.

cumulonimbus - billowing, dark storm clouds that stretch up into the sky.

cumulus - big, fluffy white clouds that form low in the sky.

dam - a barrier built across a river or stream to stop the flow.

deciduous - a tree that loses its leaves in winter.

dipping - searching for creatures in a pond, rock or tide pool or river, using a net.

embers - the hot, glowing remains of a fire after the flames have died down.

evergreen - a tree that keeps its leaves all year round.

footprint trap - a tray of sand or mud that captures the footprints of creatures who walk over it.

freshwater - water with no salt in it, found in rivers, ponds and lakes.

Full Moon - when the whole Moon is lit up in the night sky.

igloo - a traditional shelter made from bricks of compacted snow.

kindling - dry materials used to start a fire.

Land Art - a type of art that uses only natural materials.

meteorite - a space rock.

Moon - a big ball of rock that moves around the Earth.

Morse - a code in which the letters of the alphabet are turned into a series of dots and dashes of light or sound.